HEARTY
Vegetarian
Soups & Stews

Other books by Jeanne Marie Martin:

Eating Alive, co-authored with Dr. Jon Matsen
*For the Love of Food: the Complete Natural Food
    Cookbook*
The All Natural Allergy Cookbook (Harbour
    Publishing)

HEARTY
Vegetarian
Soups & Stews

JEANNE MARIE MARTIN

HARBOUR PUBLISHING

Revised and expanded edition copyright © 1991 by Jeanne
    Marie Martin
Original edition copyright © 1989 by Jeanne Marie Martin
Illustrations copyright © 1989 by Rick Dykun

Second Printing, 1992

Published by
HARBOUR PUBLISHING
P.O. Box 219
Madeira Park, BC Canada V0N 2H0

Cover design by Roger Handling
Typeset in Garth Graphic
Printed and bound in Canada

Canadian Cataloguing in Publication Data
Martin, Jeanne Marie, 1951–
    Hearty vegetarian soups & stews

    Includes index.
    ISBN 1-55017-050-3

    1. Soups.   2. Stews.   3. Vegetarian cookery.
I. Title.
TX757.M37 1991   641.8'13   C91-091383-8

For
Jennifer Weyler Kearney
with love and thanks
for her support and true friendship

Contents

Wonderful Soups   1
How to Make Wonderful Soups   2
   Making Vegetable Stock   2
   Preparing Bean Soups   3
   About All Soups   4
   About Soup Ingredients   6
Substitutions Chart for Soup Recipes   11
Product Information   13
Wonderful Soup Recipes   17
Chilled Summer Soups   71
Hearty Stews   77
Index   89

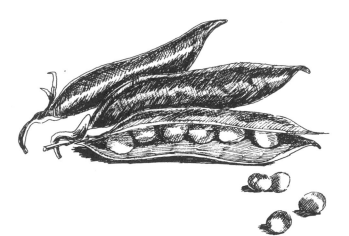

Wonderful Soups

There is nothing quite so satisfying, nourishing, or comforting on a cool day as a bowl of hot homemade soup. Serve it along with your favourite crackers, crusty bread or corn muffins. Soup is filling yet easy to digest and is low in calories and cholesterol, especially if it doesn't contain meat fats, which are used in many traditional soups for flavour. Homemade soups are also tastier and more nutritious than canned or packaged soups.

These hearty vegetarian soups require no sacrifice of flavour. A delicious blend of herbs, vegetables, whole grains, beans, miso and other special ingredients are used to enhance each soup in a unique way rather than using an old soup bone, meat chunks, regular table salt and black pepper. The wholesome ingredients used in these recipes allow the natural goodness of the soups' nutrients to be preserved, while creating flavourful and exciting new soup recipes that will tempt any tastebuds. For any age or taste, you won't have to worry about leftovers going to waste with these great soups!

Here are some tips for making expert quality soups with these or any recipes you may already treasure. The substitutions will allow you to add more flavour and nutrients to some of your own recipes. Please read this information carefully for a better understanding of what makes a perfect soup. Then feel free to explore and create your own soup recipes with all your favourite ingredients. Enjoy!

1

How to Make Wonderful Soups

Making Vegetable Stock

■ Leftover water from steaming vegetables may be used as stock.

■ Odd leftover vegetables, especially broccoli, zucchini, greens, celery, carrots, potatoes, corn, peas, beans, squash, onions, mushrooms, beets, turnips, tomatoes and cabbage can be covered in water, brought to a boil on high heat, and then simmered on low heat for 20–60 minutes. After simmering, cool and strain the mixture. Save the liquid for stock.

■ Leftover cooked vegetables can be blended or put in a food processor with water, pureed and used as stock. Use one cup vegetables for every 3 to 5 cups water.

■ Clear vegetable stock may be made using either of the first two methods above, but it must be mild-flavoured and have very little colour, or it may spoil the special flavour or colour intended for a certain soup recipe. Avoid using beets, greens or any strong coloured vegetables that may dye the water a dark colour.

Preparing Bean Soups

1. Soak the beans (legumes) in water overnight or for 8 hours or more. Soak 1 cup of dry beans in 3 to 4 cups of water.

2. Discard the beans' soaking water, and rinse the beans several times thoroughly with fresh water.

3. Bring the beans, along with the amount of fresh water indicated in each recipe, to a boil on high heat.

4. Scoop off and discard any froth or foam in the water that rises to the top as the beans come to a boil.

5. Turn the heat down to low and cook for 1 to 2 hours until the beans are tender enough to be mashed easily on the roof of your mouth with your tongue.

6. Add extra water if necessary (because of evaporation) so the soup contains the full amount of water required in the recipe.

7. Proceed with the soup recipe.

About All Soups

1. Never boil soups. This destroys nutrients and flavours. Simmer them on low to medium heat.

2. Never add cold milk or cream to a hot pan or to other hot ingredients. Heat the milk before adding to something hot. Cold added to hot may splash out of the pan!

3. Good soups should be a blend of flavours with no single ingredient overpowering the others.

4. If too much sea salt or another herb or spice is added to a soup, add extra water, stock, or milk, *or* add a starchy vegetable, noodle, flour or whole grain. This will absorb excess sea salt and some other seasonings as well.

5. Cool a soup completely before putting it into containers. This helps prevent quick spoilage and avoids pressure buildup in the closed container. It also keeps metal lids from rusting and discourages the absorption of plastic into hot foods when plastic storage containers are used.

6. Always freeze cooled soups in plastic containers filled only ¾ full so there is room for the soup to expand as it freezes. Don't freeze in glass as it allows no room for expansion and easily breaks. Most soups may be frozen for three months or more.

7. Most soups lose little flavour when frozen. However, if flavour is lost, add a bit of tamari, miso, or herbs to perk up the taste.

8. Because there are low- and high-salt tamaris, and salted and unsalted butter and bouillon cubes, salt amounts in recipes may vary greatly. If you are not using low-salt products, or if you are on a low-salt diet, use less than the amount called for in the recipe, and adjust according to personal taste.

About Soup Ingredients

Sea salt: Brings out all other flavours in the soup and enhances them. Amounts can sometimes be cut back or substituted for special diets. Vegetable powders and other herbs reduce the need for much salt. Sea salt is better than regular table salt because it doesn't contain sugar, whiteners, and other extenders. ¾ teaspoon sea salt equals 1 teaspoon table salt.

Sea kelp: Adds body and depth to soups and main dishes and is also high in iodine and other trace minerals. The right amount gives the soup a lovely base and a bit of a robust background flavour. Too much in a soup may make it taste a little "muddy." Several dashes, or ¼ to ½ teaspoon, is used in most soups.

Tamari soy sauce: Adds sea salt and gives body and depth to recipes, a heartier, slightly bouillon-like flavour. Real soy sauce is called tamari because it is naturally aged and fermented for 6 months to 2 years, usually in wood, and it does not contain harmful, artificial additives like caramel colouring and MSG.

Miso: Another fermented soybean product that contains healing enzymes and nutrients and some sea salt. It gives body to soup and can be used almost by itself with water, a few green onions, or spinach. Never overheat or boil it as this destroys the beneficial enzymes.

Honey or other sweeteners: Another very special aid to enhancing the soups' taste and bringing out the other ingredients' flavours. A touch of sweetener in a soup, usually 1–2 teaspoons, has a balancing effect on the other ingredients. Just as salt brings out the sweetness in a cake, honey or another sweetener brings out the seasonings in a main dish or soup. Opposites complement each other!

Milk or cream: Adds richness (and calories) to soup. It is a wonderful addition to luxurious soups, yet can detract from the flavour of some soups. Try recipes with and without and note the difference in flavours. Those with food allergies will appreciate the Substitutions Chart on pages 11 and 12. Some recipes require dairy milk, others mention substitutions if they can be used in that recipe.

Vegetable stock, vegetable bouillon cubes and vegetable broth powder: Delicious bases for most soups. These enrich the flavour of other ingredients but are not enough on their own to completely flavour soups. Many of these are salt-free and low calorie.

Flours or arrowroot powder: These help thicken soups and improve the taste, especially if the flour has been browned in butter, making what is called a roux.

Herbs: Are usually green, leafy parts of plants and sometimes seeds. Examples are: parsley, marjoram, basil, oregano, thyme, dill and cumin. Herbs add minerals, nutrients, and flavour to soups. They enhance the flavour of vegetables, grains, and beans, can aid digestion, and are healing for the body. They can be used generously in most recipes as they are beneficial. Herb amounts used in all recipes are dried herbs.

Spices: Are usually barks, roots, and strong seeds. Examples are: cinnamon, nutmeg, mustard, black and white pepper, tumeric, cardamon and coriander. Spices are avoided in most of these recipes as they are irritants to the body (especially the stomach) and deter healing. Small amounts are acceptable if used only occasionally.

Cayenne pepper: Better than black pepper, which is a spice. Cayenne is beneficial and healing to the body. It helps the circulation, mildly stimulates the heart and aids in thinning the blood. Red pepper also helps eliminate congestion and breaks up mucus in the body. Cayenne is a spicy vegetable seasoning that, used sparingly, gives just the right "kick" to soups. However, don't overuse it or you may spoil a soup by making it too spicy. Several dashes to $\frac{1}{16}$ teaspoon medium hot cayenne is usually enough for most soups. Use more if the cayenne is very mild. Sprinkle on soups, mix well, cook for 5 or more minutes, and taste before adding extra so as not to overuse.

Onions and garlic: Add zesty flavour and have healing qualities. Fresh garlic, especially, helps prevent illness and destroys bacteria. One or two cloves of crushed garlic may be added to many soups either raw, sautéed, or simmered. Two to three teaspoons raw, crushed onion is equal to 1 small cooked onion in soups. Onions can also be raw, sautéed (for more flavour), or simmered in a soup. Use 1 to 2 small to medium onions for most soups.

Vegetables: Are the main base for many soups and are high in nutrients, vitamins, minerals, and flavour. Each vegetable adds special properties and taste(s) to a soup which may vary according to how the vegetable is cooked before adding it: either sautéed, steamed or simmered.

Starchy vegetables, whole grains and noodles: A main ingredient in many soups. Many of these do not add much flavour, but they do add texture, carbohydrates, and nutrients. More seasonings are required in soups containing one or more of these. If a soup happens to be overspiced, potatoes, noodles, or whole grains will often absorb and dilute the excess spices.

Legumes (beans, peas and lentils): An important ingredient in some soups. These are high in protein, calcium, iron and many other nutrients. Some have a subtle flavour, like chick peas, soybeans and navy beans. Others, such as kidney beans, pintos, adukis (also spelled azuki or adzuki) or brown lentils, create a gravy-like base that enriches the quality and taste of the soup. Make sure they are cooked very tender so that the nutrients are assimilated and the legumes can be easily digested.

Butter or natural oil: Good for sautéing. One or both of these in a soup gives a richer flavour and adds quality as well as a few extra calories. Unrefined, cold-pressed safflower or sunflower oils are among the best oils to use in soup recipes. See the Product Information page (page 13) for more about oils.

Substitutions Chart for Soup Recipes

INSTEAD OF:	USE:
Meat juices, ham or meat bones for flavour	Tamari soy sauce, vegetable bouillon cubes, vegetable broth powder, sea kelp, vegetable stock, herbs, miso
Sugar (or honey)	Maple syrup, unsulphured molasses, raw sugar, malt or another sweetener
White (or whole wheat) flour	Millet, oat, barley, buckwheat, corn or amaranth flour *or* arrowroot powder
Cornstarch (hinders digestion)	Arrowroot powder (in same proportions)
Butter	Mild-flavoured, cold-pressed, unrefined oil (safflower or sunflower are best)
Milk or cream	Soy, cashew, blanched almond or seed milk *or* 7 oz. water and 2 Tbs butter per 1 cup milk or cream (Note: These substitutions cannot be used in all recipes instead of dairy. Some recipes require dairy where specified.)

INSTEAD OF:	USE:
Table salt (regular)	Sea salt – use ¾ tsp sea salt per l tsp regular table salt (Some salt substitutes are available – See Product Information)
Dried herbs	Fresh herbs – use ¼ cup fresh herbs per 2–3 tsp of the same dried herb. These recipes call for dried herbs unless otherwise specified.
Tamari soy sauce	Quick Sip (brand name) – unsalted soy sauce substitute, miso (See Product Information)
Worcestershire sauce	Tamari mixed with honey and apple cider vinegar – use about 4 tsp tamari and l tsp each honey and vinegar per 2 Tbs Worcestershire, or varied amounts
Black pepper	Cayenne pepper – use several dashes or $\frac{1}{16}$ to $\frac{1}{8}$ tsp medium cayenne pepper per l tsp black (use ½ to 1 tsp mild cayenne per l tsp black)
Mushrooms	Eggplant sautéed in a bit of oil and tamari until very tender

Product Information
Recommended ingredients and brand name products

Product	Brand names	Special benefit or use
Apple cider vinegar	Lifestream, Canasoy	Natural brands, naturally processed, have better flavour
Beans (canned)	Unico, Primo	When dried are unavailable or time is short, these may sometimes be used, though they are less nutritious. However, these brands are sugar-free, unlike some others. (Note: Rinse canned beans thoroughly before using in recipes.)
Bouillon cubes (vegetable)	Bio-Force (Hugli), Morga	Vegetarian, natural flavour base for soups

Product	Brand names	Special benefit or use
Herbs	Golden Bough, Sun Isle, Folklore, Gayelord Hauser's Spike brand	Natural and organic, high-quality herbs have richer flavours and aromas
Miso	Westbrae, Amano	Natural miso without added chemicals or additives found in some oriental and commercial brands
Oils, cold-pressed, unrefined	Flora, Purity Life, Spectrum, Lifestream, Eden, Vita-Health	Use these high-quality natural oils for cooking: sunflower, safflower and sesame. Avoid commercial processed oils.
Salt substitutes	Potassium chloride, Gayelord Hauser's Santay-Garlic Magic and Vegit	Use potassium chloride sparingly in some recipes about ¼ tsp per each 1 tsp sea salt. Experiment with other salt-free seasonings

Product	Brand names	Special benefit or use
Seaweeds	Fresh – Canasoy (sometimes) Dried – Westbrae	Since fresh are rarely available in many areas, dried may be used in smaller quantities. Seaweeds add nutrients and enzymes as well as flavour
Special seasoning mixtures	Bio-Force – Herbamare, Gayelord Hauser – Vege-Sal & Spike, Future Produces Inc. – Zhug	For extra flavour enhancement of soups that seem a little bland or need an extra boost of flavour
Tamari soy sauce	San-j, Eden, Amano, Lifestream, Canasoy, Westbrae	These high-quality tamaris are naturally processed. San-j and Eden are low-salt varieties and some are wheat-free
Tamari soy sauce substitute	Bernard Jensen's Quick Sip	Similar to tamari in aging and flavour but made with added dulse, calcium and potassium – ant it's completely salt-free. A bouillon concentrate

Product	Brand names	Special benefit or use
Vegetables (dried)	Canasoy and some bulk food companies	Convienient, yet less nutritious than fresh vegetables, for adding to minestrone, vegetable and some other soups
Vegetable broth powders	Bernard Jensen's Hidden Valley, Gayelord Hauser, Canasoy, Hugli	These may be used with or instead of bouillon cubes for flavour and to give body to soups. They must be cooked at least 20 minutes in recipes for the best flavour
Vegetable or vegetized sea salt	Canasoy	Can be used raw or cooked in foods. Flavours instantly. Tastes better than just plain salt or sea salt. Also contains powdered spinach, carrot, alfalfa, celery and green peas

Wonderful Soup Recipes

Vegetable Tomato Soup
(Serves 8–10)

6–7 cups	water *or* vegetable stock
1 cup	fresh or frozen peas *or* chopped green beans
1 cup	mushrooms, sliced
3–4	large tomatoes, chopped, *or* 1 medium or large can of tomatoes, cored and crushed (The liquid part from the canned tomatoes may be used as part of the vegetable stock.)
2	medium potatoes, unpeeled and cut into small chunks
2–3	stalks celery *or* 1 green pepper, chopped
2	carrots, thinly sliced
1	large onion, chopped
Optional:	1 cup corn, fresh or frozen
1–2 Tbs	unrefined, cold-pressed oil
1–2 Tbs	tamari soy sauce
2–3 tsp	vegetable broth powder *or* 2 vegetable bouillon cubes
2–3 tsp	parsley
1–1½ tsp	sea salt
½ tsp each	basil, oregano, and sea kelp Cayenne pepper to taste
Optional:	1–2 tsp honey *or* other sweetener

Steam the potatoes and carrots for 6–8 minutes before making the soup.

Sauté the onions and mushrooms in the oil in a large pot until they are slightly transparent. Add the water or stock, steamed vegetables, and remaining vegetables and cook for 30 minutes on low to medium heat. After adding the herbs and other ingredients, cook another 30 minutes until the vegetables are tender but not soggy and the flavours have developed.

Correct the herbs according to personal taste and add extra water if needed. Add ½ cup dry alphabet noodles or other noodles during the last 30 minutes of cooking time, if desired. Serve hot with your favourite crackers.

Keeps 6–7 days refrigerated. It is preferable not to freeze this soup as most of the nutrients will be lost.

Vegetable Broth

Use 1–2 cups leftover VEGETABLE SOUP or MISO SOUP and liquefy in a blender or food processor. Add extra leftover steamed vegetables if desired, using extra water to thin the broth to a desired consistency. Additional flavourings can be added if necessary. Heat on medium-low heat for 15–30 minutes and serve hot or cold in a bowl or glass.

Vegetable Soup
(without tomatoes or mushrooms)
(Serves 6-8)

6-7 cups   water *or* vegetable stock
1 cup   fresh or frozen peas *or* chopped green beans
1 cup   fresh or frozen corn (may be sliced off the cob)
1-2   potatoes *or* jerusalem artichokes, unpeeled and cut into small chunks
2-3   stalks celery *or* 1 green pepper, chopped
2   carrots, thinly sliced
1   large onion
1   small zucchini, thinly sliced or chopped
1   stalk broccoli

1-2 Tbs   unrefined, cold-pressed oil
1-2 Tbs   tamari soy sauce
3-4 tsp   vegetable broth powder *or* 3-4 vegetable bouillon cubes
2-3 tsp   parsley
1½ tsp   sea salt
½ tsp each   basil, oregano and sea kelp
Several dashes   cayenne pepper
Optional: A bit of honey
Optional: Dark miso – keep separate

Steam the potatoes and carrots for 10 minutes before making the soup.
Sauté the onions in the oil in a large pot until they

are slightly transparent. Then add the water and all the rest of the ingredients, including the steamed vegetables.

Cook the soup on low-to-medium heat for 40–60 minutes until all the vegetables are tender but not soggy and the flavours are developed.

Take 1–2 cups of water with some vegetables from the soup and blend it or use a food processor to liquefy and add it back into the soup. This adds flavour and depth and gives the soup a natural thickness. Correct the soup's spices according to personal taste and add a bit of honey to balance the flavours if desired, or add extra water to thin the soup.

After the soup is finished cooking, 1–2 Tbs miso can also be blended with one cup of the broth and then added back to the soup for more taste and nutritional value.

Keeps refrigerated for 6–7 days. Do not freeze.

Easy Miso Soup

(Serves 6–8)

> 1 tsp sesame oil (regular or toasted)
> 2–3 green onions, chopped small
>
> 4 cups water
> ¼ cup dark miso
> 1 Tbs tamari soy sauce
> ⅛ tsp sea kelp
>   Cayenne pepper to taste
>
> 2–3 oz tofu, diced into ⅛" cubes
> *Optional:* 10–16 leaves spinach *or* 2–6
>   leaves chard, chopped

Sauté the green onion in the oil then add all the remaining ingredients *except* for the tofu and greens. Use a wire whisk to help mix in the miso while mixing over medium-low heat. When the miso has dissolved, add the tofu and greens and let everything simmer on low heat for 8–12 minutes until the greens are tender. Correct the seasonings as desired. Serve hot. Keeps 3–6 days refrigerated. Do not freeze. Don't allow the soup to boil at any time especially while reheating.

Miso Soup
(Serves 4–8)

6 cups	water *or* vegetable stock
1–2 oz	dried seaweed *or* 4 oz fresh (wakame or kombu are best), rinsed and sliced
1	large onion, chopped
2	carrots, thinly sliced
2–4	stalks celery, chopped
1–2	vegetable bouillon cubes *or* 1–2 tsp vegetable broth powder
1–2 Tbs	unrefined, cold-pressed oil
1–2 tsp	parsley
½ tsp	sea salt
Several dashes	sea kelp
⅓ cup	dark miso (brown rice or soy miso are good) – keep separate

Sauté the onions and vegetables in the oil in a pot big enough to hold all the soup. When the vegetables are tender and the onions are slightly transparent, add the water, seaweed, and all the rest of the soup ingredients (except the miso). Let the soup cook, covered, for about 25–35 minutes.

Remove the soup from the heat, take 1 cup of broth from the soup, and stir the miso into it. When the miso is dissolved into the broth, mix it with the rest of the soup and leave covered (away from heat) about 5–10 minutes so the flavours can mingle. Do not cook the miso; this destroys valuable vitamins and enzymes. Serve the soup immediately when ready. Leftover soup can be reheated slightly, but never let it boil.

Keeps refrigerated for 5–6 days. Do not freeze.

Pinto Bean Soup (or Aduki Soup)
(Serves 10–12)

2 cups	dry pinto beans *or* aduki beans, soaked and cooked (2 cups dry beans makes 5 cups cooked)
10–12 cups	water *or* vegetable stock
1	large onion, finely chopped
2–3 Tbs	tamari soy sauce
2 Tbs	parsley
2 Tbs	butter *or* 1–2 Tbs unrefined, cold-pressed oil
4 tsp	vegetable broth powder
2	bouillon cubes
½–1 tsp	sea salt *or* vegetable salt
½–¾ tsp	sea kelp
	Cayenne pepper to taste
Optional:	1–2 tsp honey *or* other sweetener

3–4 Tbs dark miso – keep separate

Read the tips at the beginning of this book on preparing bean soups (page 3). Cook the pinto beans until tender. After cooking, add enough water or stock to total 10 cups of liquid. Add the onion and cook for 20 minutes. Then add the remaining ingredients (except the miso) and cook another 20 minutes more on medium heat.

Take 2–4 cups of beans and liquid from the soup, blend or process into liquid, and re-add it to the soup. Next, take out 1 more cup of the liquid from the soup and mix the miso into it, stirring it carefully to break down any lumps before adding the miso liquid to the soup.

1–2 cups extra hot water may be added to the soup after the miso if a thinner, milder soup is desired. Serve hot and enjoy.

Keeps well 7–8 days refrigerated and freezes wonderfully. An easy to digest and highly nutritious soup!

Black Bean Soup
(Serves 10–12)

10 cups	water *or* vegetable stock
2 cups	dry black beans, soaked and cooked (2 cups dry beans makes 5 cups cooked)
1	large onion, chopped
2	cloves garlic, minced
2	carrots, finely grated
2	stalks celery, finely chopped
3 Tbs	dried parsley
3 Tbs	molasses (Barbados), unsulphured
2–3 Tbs	tamari soy sauce
1–2 Tbs	unrefined, cold-pressed oil
3	bouillon cubes
2 tsp each	cumin and coriander
1 tsp	sea salt
½ tsp	ground cloves
Several dashes	sea kelp
	Cayenne pepper to taste

Read the tips at the beginning of this book on preparing bean soups (page 3). Once the black beans are soaked and cooked, add enough water so the beans are covered by ½ inch or so (about 10 cups).

In a large skillet, heat the oil on medium high heat and sauté the onion, garlic, carrots, celery, and parsley until very tender. Then add the sautéed mixture to the beans along with the remaining ingredients. Cook everything together for 15–20 minutes to blend the flavours. Correct the seasonings as desired and serve hot. Garnish with chopped, fresh parsley, green onions, alfalfa sprouts, or chives.

Keeps 7–8 days refrigerated and freezes well. Black beans are exceptionally high in many nutrients including protein, phosphorus, potassium, calcium, and iron.

Fasoulada Bean Soup (Greek)

(Serves 6–8)

2 cups	dry navy *or* white beans, soaked and cooked
2 cups	water
1	795 mL (28 oz.) can tomatoes, cored
6–12 oz	tomato juice
4 stalks	celery, chopped small
3	carrots, chopped small
1	big onion, chopped or diced
2	cloves garlic, minced
2	vegetable bouillon cubes
2–4 Tbs	olive oil
2 Tbs	tamari soy sauce
2–3 tsp	honey, maple syrup *or* fruit concentrate
1–1½ tsp	sea salt
½ tsp each	sea kelp and paprika
	Cayenne pepper to taste
Optional:	1 leek *or* 1–3 green onions, chopped

While the beans are cooking, chop the vegetables and add them to beans during the last ½ hour the beans cook. When the beans are tender, drain all the liquid from the beans and measure 2 cups of liquid back into the beans. Add extra water if needed for a thinner consistency. Blend the tomatoes with all the herbs, spices and bouillon cubes. Mix the blended mixture with the beans, tomato juice, honey and oil and simmer everything on low heat for 20–30 minutes until flavours mingle. Enjoy hot or cool and store. Keeps 6–8 days refrigerated or may be frozen.

Hearty Mung Bean Soup

(Serves 8)

4 cups	water *or* stock
1 cup	dry, green mung beans (*not* mung bean sprouts)
4–5	large tomatoes, chopped, *or* 1 795 mL (28 oz.) can tomatoes, chopped
1	large onion, chopped
2	vegetable bouillon cubes
2 Tbs	tamari soy sauce
2 Tbs	dried parsley
2–4 tsp	honey *or* other sweetener
1 tsp	basil
¹⁄₁₆–⅛ tsp	cayenne pepper to taste
Several dashes	sea kelp
Optional:	Sea salt or vegetable sea salt to taste
Optional:	5–6 oz tomato paste

Sort the mung beans carefully and discard broken or misshapen beans. Wash the beans and bring them to a boil on high heat with the 4 cups water or stock. Simmer the beans for ½ hour, then add the tomatoes and cook another ½ hour. Add the onions and cook for another ½ hour until the beans have cooked approximately 90 minutes and are very tender through and through. Stir occasionally. Add all the remaining ingredients and cook another 15–20 minutes until the flavours mingle. A small can (5–6 oz) of tomato paste may be added at this time if desired for a more tomatoey taste.

Keeps 7–8 days refrigerated and freezes well.

Green and Red Mung Bean Soup

(Serves 8–10)

Follow the directions for Hearty Mung Bean Soup (above), but:

> *Omit:* 2 Tbs dried parsley
> *Add:* 1 bunch green onion tops, green part only, chopped
> ½–1 bunch spinach *or* chard, chopped
> sea salt *or* vegetable sea salt to taste
> ½–1 cup chopped fresh parsley
> the optional 5–6 oz tomato paste

Lentil Soup

(Serves 5-6)

4½–5 cups	water *or* stock
1 cup	dry brown (green) lentils
4–6	stalks celery (or 2–3 stalks broccoli), chopped
2	carrots, sliced
1	large onion, chopped
1–2	cloves garlic, minced
2 Tbs	butter *or* unrefined, cold-pressed oil
2 Tbs	tamari soy sauce
3 tsp	parsley
1 tsp each	sea salt and vegetable broth powder
½ tsp each	basil, oregano and thyme
⅛ tsp	cayenne pepper
Several dashes	sea kelp
Optional:	½ tsp dill weed

Bring the dry lentils, vegetables, and water or stock to a boil on high heat, then simmer for 1 hour on low heat or until the lentils are very tender. Add the remaining ingredients and simmer another 15–20 minutes, stirring occasionally. Serve hot and enjoy.

Keeps 7 days in the refrigerator or may be frozen for later use.

Lentil Tomato Soup
(Serves 8–10)

8 cups	water *or* vegetable stock*
2 cups	dry brown lentils
1	13 oz (369 mL) can of tomato paste
3–4	large tomatoes, chopped *or* 1 large can (795 mL or 28 oz) tomatoes with juice, cored and chopped
3–4	stalks celery, chopped
1	large onion, chopped
1–2 Tbs	tamari soy sauce
2 tsp	parsley
1–2 tsp	honey (or other sweetener)
1 tsp each	sea salt, basil, and oregano
½ tsp each	sea kelp, marjoram and thyme
Several dashes	cayenne pepper

Cook the lentils and water for 30 minutes in a large pot on medium heat. Add the onions, tomatoes, and vegetables and cook for another 30 minutes or more. When the lentils are very tender, add the herbs and remaining ingredients and continue cooking everything on low heat for about 20–25 minutes of until the tomatoes have turned to liquid and the vegetables are tender. Keep stirring the soup occasionally.

*For a more stew-like consistency, omit about 1 cup of the water or stock.

Will stay fresh up to 7 days refrigerated or may be frozen.

Split Pea Soup
(Serves 8–10)

1 lb	(2¼–2½ cups) dry green split peas
7–9 cups	water *or* vegetable stock
2	medium onions, very finely chopped
¼ cup	butter *or* 1–2 Tbs unrefined, cold-pressed oil
3–5 tsp	tamari soy sauce
2 tsp	parsley
1½ tsp	sea salt
1–2 tsp	honey
1 tsp each	basil, oregano and mint leaves, crushed
½ tsp each	thyme and sea kelp
¼ tsp each	marjoram and savory
Several dashes	cayenne pepper to taste
Optional:	1–2 potatoes and/or carrots, finely chopped and pre-steamed 7–10 minutes before adding with the onions

Swirl the split peas around by hand in a large pan of water, changing the water several times, to remove the bubbly liquid from the peas, which can cause gas. Drain the water off, then add the 7–9 cups fresh water or stock the recipe requires.

Cook the dry split peas and water in a large pot for 1½ to 2 hours on medium heat or until the peas completely dissolve into the liquid. Stir occasionally. Then add the onions, herbs, and vegetables (if any), butter or oil, and cook over a low to medium heat for 20–25 minutes more to develop the flavours. Keep stirring the soup occasionally, leaving the heat low so it simmers and does not stick or burn.

Each serving may be topped with a bit of chopped green onion or a small handful of alfalfa sprouts. Keeps refrigerated 6–7 days and may be frozen.

Minestrone Soup
(Serves 12–14)

8 cups	water *or* vegetable stock
8	large *or* 12 medium fresh, ripe tomatoes, finely chopped *or* 2 cans (598 mL or 21 oz) tomatoes, cored and crushed with juice
¾ cup	dry kidney beans, soaked and cooked (makes 2¼ cups)
¾ cup	dry chick peas, soaked and cooked (makes 2¼ cups)
1	very large *or* 2 medium onions, chopped
1½ cups	celery, chopped
1	small zucchini, quartered and chopped
2–3	carrots, diced very finely
3 Tbs	tamari soy sauce
2 Tbs	oil (olive oil may be used if desired, or any natural oil)
2	vegetable bouillon cubes
2 tsp	sea salt
2	cloves garlic, crushed
	Cayenne pepper to taste
Optional:	⅔ cup grated parmesan cheese
Optional:	½ cup dry elbow *or* alphabet noodles, pre-cooked, *or* 1–2 cups pre-cooked rice *or* barley
Optional:	1 tsp of one or more of the following: parsley, basil or oregano

Sauté the onion in oil and add the water and vegetables. Simmer for about 40 minutes or until the vegetables are tender. Add the pre- cooked beans, any extra herbs, and the remaining ingredients (except for the optionals), and cook for another 20 minutes or so. The parmesan and noodles or grain can then be added if desired. Serve hot when ready.

Keeps 7–8 days refrigerated. May be frozen, though it's not recommended.

Onion Soup
(Serves 4–6)

6 cups	white *or* yellow onions, cut in half and very thinly sliced
4 cups	water *or* clear vegetable stock
6–8 Tbs	butter
2 Tbs	tamari soy sauce
1	small clove garlic, crushed
1	vegetable bouillon cube
½–1 tsp	sea salt
½ tsp	dry mustard
⅛ tsp	thyme
Several dashes	sea kelp
Optional:	Bread *or* croutons
Optional:	Swiss, cheddar *or* parmesan cheese

Sauté the onions in the butter on medium heat for about 30–40 minutes until they are slightly brown and very tender and transparent. Add the remaining ingredients and mix thoroughly. Cook an additional 30 minutes, covered, on low to medium heat. Serve topped with rounds of toasted bread or croutons and grated cheddar or parmesan cheese. A slice of cheddar or Swiss cheese can also be melted over individual onion soup crocks.

Best if eaten within 5–6 days. Do not freeze.

Mushroom Soup
(Serves 4)

4 cups	mushrooms, sliced or chopped
2 Tbs	butter *or* oil
2¼ cups	milk *or* nut milk
3–5 tsp	light miso
Optional:	couple of dashes cayenne pepper
3–4 cups	regular, oyster or shitake mushrooms, sliced or chopped
1	large stalk celery, chopped small
2 Tbs	butter *or* oil

Sauté the 4 cups mushrooms in 2 Tbs butter or oil until very tender. Blend the sautéed mushrooms with the milk, miso and cayenne. Sauté the remaining three ingredients in a medium saucepan until tender but not too soft. Add the blended mixture to the saucepan and simmer everything on low heat until hot throughout. Correct the seasonings as desired. Serve and enjoy. Keeps 2–4 days. Do not freeze.

Dried Mushroom Soup

(Serves 2)

1½ cups	dried mushrooms
2 cups	water for heating
1½ cups	water for soaking
1 cup	half-and-half *or* ⅓ cup cream and
	⅔ cup milk
1	vegetable bouillon cube
2 Tbs	whole wheat flour
1–2 tsp	chopped white onion
1–2 tsp	tamari soy sauce
Optional:	few dashes cayenne pepper

Put the dried mushrooms and 2 cups of water into a medium saucepan and bring them up to a full boil on medium-high heat. Remove from the heat at once and swish the mushrooms in the hot water to loosen any dirt on the mushrooms. Use a slotted spoon to remove the mushrooms from the water. Rinse the mushrooms again in warm water if necessary. Then soak the mushrooms in 1½ cups fresh water for 4–8 hours until softened. Chop the mushrooms into small pieces and simmer them in their soaking water for 15–20 minutes, on medium heat, until very tender. Blend the remaining ingredients and add them to the mushrooms. Cook everything for another 10–12 minutes on low heat until the soup thickens a bit. Stir occasionally. Serve hot with crusty bread for dipping. This elegant soup keeps 3–5 days refrigerated. Do not freeze.

Borscht

(Serves 8-10)

4 cups	water from steamed vegetables
4 cups	cabbage, shredded
2 cups	beets, chopped or sliced
1 cup	potatoes, chopped in small cubes
1 cup	tomato purée
½ cup	carrot (about 1 medium), thinly sliced
2	large onions (about 1½ - 2 cups), finely chopped
1½-2 Tbs	apple cider vinegar
1½-2 Tbs	honey (same amount as vinegar)
1 Tbs	vegetable broth powder *or* 2 vegetable bouillon cubes
1-1½ tsp	sea salt
3	bay leaves
¼ tsp	dill weed
	Cayenne pepper to taste
3 Tbs	butter *or* unrefined, cold-pressed oil
Optional Toppings:	chopped tomatoes, chives or fresh parsley and/or sour cream or yogurt

Steam the beets, potatoes, and carrot until tender, and save the steaming water. Add extra water to the steaming water to equal 4 cups stock and put aside.

In a soup pot, sauté the onions in hot butter or oil until semi-tender. Add the cabbage and sauté another 5-8 minutes until the cabbage is fairly tender. Add the 4 cups steamed vegetable water and the steamed beets, potatoes, and carrot. Then put in the rest of the ingredients (except the toppings), stir, cover, and let simmer on low heat for about 30 minutes.

Remove the bay leaves and adjust the flavour if desired. Serve hot with topping(s). Keeps refrigerated 5–6 days. This soup best if not frozen.

Corn Chowder
(Serves 8-10)

3-4 Tbs	butter *or* unrefined, cold-pressed oil
1	medium or large onion, finely chopped
⅔ cup	celery, finely chopped
⅔ cup	green pepper, finely chopped
4 cups	fresh or frozen corn
2 cups	water
2 cups	milk
3-4 Tbs	whole wheat flour *or* other flour
2 Tbs	butter
2 Tbs	tamari soy sauce
1-2 Tbs	vegetable broth powder
1 tsp each	sea salt and paprika
¼ tsp	sea kelp
	Cayenne pepper to taste

In a medium sized soup pot, sauté the onion in oil or butter until slightly tender. Add the celery and green pepper and sauté for another 2-3 minutes. Next, add the water and corn and simmer for 15-20 minutes, covered. The milk, extra butter, and the remaining ingredients can then be added, using a wire whisk if necessary to make sure the flour and herbs are mixed in completely. Simmer another 20 minutes, serve and enjoy.

The chowder keeps up to 7-8 days refrigerated. Leftovers may be frozen.

Cream of Asparagus Soup
(Serves 4-6)

1¼ lb (570 g)	fresh asparagus
5 cups	vegetable steaming water
1 cup	cream
4-6	small green onions, chopped
½ cup	celery, chopped
3 Tbs	butter
3 Tbs	whole wheat flour (or other – see Substitutions Chart, page 11)
1 tsp	sea salt
½ tsp	paprika
Several dashes	cayenne pepper

Wash the asparagus and trim off about ⅓ of the tough bottom of each stalk making sure to remove all white parts. Choose thin, young asparagus with firm tips. The bottoms of the asparagus can be discarded or, if green, may be peeled carefully and the inner part may be used in the soup. Steam the trimmed asparagus until tender.

In a skillet, sauté the onion and celery in butter until tender and blend or process the mixture with the asparagus and the remaining ingredients. Heat everything in a double boiler or saucepan on very low heat for 10-15 minutes until hot throughout to let the flavours mingle. Do not boil. Serve immediately, and enjoy a rich and flavourful soup.

Keeps 3-5 days refrigerated. Do not freeze.

Spinach Soup
(Serves 4)

1¼ lbs (570 g)	fresh spinach
2 cups	milk *or* milk substitute
1–2	green onions, chopped
1	small clove garlic, minced
1–2 tsp	tamari soy sauce
½ tsp	sea salt (or a bit more)
½ tsp	basil
¼ tsp	thyme
Several dashes	sea kelp
	Cayenne pepper to taste
Optional:	Home-roasted slivered almonds or other nuts

Roux:

4 Tbs	butter
4 Tbs	whole wheat *or* other flour

Carefully wash the spinach by swishing it in a bowl or sinkful of water to remove all the sand and grit. Steam the spinach, and then blend it with all the ingredients except the butter and flour.

To make the roux, melt the butter on medium heat in a large saucepan and add the flour, stirring while it browns for several minutes. Then add the blended mixture to the saucepan and heat just up to boiling. Serve hot with slivered almonds or other chopped nuts or seeds as a garnish. The nuts are best if purchased raw and "home-roasted."

The soup keeps 3–5 days refrigerated. Do not freeze.

Parsley Soup
(Serves 4–6)

4 cups	unpeeled white potatoes, cut in ½″ cubes
1 cup	water
1 bunch	spinach leaves
1½ cups	nut milk *or* milk
1 cup	lightly chopped fresh parsley
1–2 Tbs	butter *or* cold-pressed oil
1	vegetable bouillon cube
1 tsp	vegetable broth powder
2–3 Tbs	tamari soy sauce
2–3 tsp	chopped white onion
1 tsp *each:*	paprika and basil
	Vegetable sea salt to taste
1 cup	very finely chopped parsley (at least twice as fine as the previous amount!)

Rinse the potato several times to remove excess starch before cooking. Simmer the potato in the water for 10 minutes or until tender. After the potatoes have been cooking for 2–3 minutes, add the spinach leaves on top of them and continue simmering, covered, until tender, about 7–10 minutes longer.

Blend the simmered vegetables and any remaining cooking water with all the other ingredients *except* the 1 cup finely chopped parsley. Put the blended soup mixture in a medium saucepan and stir in the finely chopped parsley. Bring the mixture just up to a boil and let it simmer on low heat for 10–15 minutes as the flavours mingle. Correct the seasoning as desired. Serve garnished with extra sprigs of parsley or chopped green onion tops. Keeps fresh for 3–6 days, refrigerated. Do not freeze.

Kale Soup

(Serves 3-4)

2 small bunches	*or* 1 large bunch kale (about 12-16 large leaves)
2 cups	nut *or* soy milk
1 Tbs	cold-pressed oil *or* butter
1	vegetable bouillon cube
¼ tsp	sea salt *or* ⅓-½ tsp vegetable sea salt
2-3 tsp	tamari soy sauce
Few dashes each:	cayenne pepper and sea kelp
Optional:	1-2 Tbs whole wheat or other flour
Optional:	pine nuts *or* slivered almonds as a garnish

Wash and trim the kale leaves. Lightly chop ⅔ of the leaves (about 10-11 leaves) and steam them for 7-10 minutes until tender. Then put the steamed kale in the blender with all the remaining ingredients *except* the 4-5 extra kale leaves. Blend thoroughly. Remove the entire stems from the remaining kale leaves, chop them very fine and steam them for 5-8 minutes until tender. Combine the blended mixture and the finely chopped, steamed kale in a saucepan. Bring them up to boiling on ow heat and simmer 5-10 minutes so the flavours develop. Serve hot garnished with pine nuts (pignolias) or slivered almonds for the added taste appeal and extra protein. Keeps 3-5 days refrigerated. Do not freeze.

"Home-Roasted" Nuts

Chopped or slivered nuts may be roasted in a dry pan at 300° for 4–8 minutes, depending on the size of the nuts and how thinly they are layered. Stir them every minute or so and turn them as needed until lightly browned and hot.

Use as a garnish for soups and other recipes. Store in the refrigerator. They keep for several weeks. Roast whole nuts at 350° for 6–10 minutes, almonds at 400° for 8–10 minutes.

Nut Milk

> 3–4 Tbs raw cashew pieces *or* raw
> blanched almonds
> 1½ cups water

Blend thoroughly in the blender or a food processor for 2–4 minutes at the highest speed until the water becomes white with the blended nuts. Strain if needed and use in many recipes instead of cow's milk. Use only in recipes where suggested, or the recipe may need to be altered to achieve a good flavour.

Broccoli or Zucchini Soup
(Serves 3–4)

3–4	stalks broccoli (about 4 cups), chopped for steaming *or* 3–4 small zucchini (about 4 cups), chopped
1½ cups	cashew *or* blanched almond milk
2–3 tsp	parsley
½ tsp	basil
¼–½ tsp	sea salt
¼ tsp *each*	thyme and paprika
Several dashes	cayenne pepper
Optional:	1–3 tsp tamari soy sauce
Optional:	For Zucchini Soup *only*: add a few spinach leaves or ¼ to ½ tsp dill weed or tarragon

Use high quality broccoli or zucchini as it is very important to the flavour of the soup.

Steam the vegetables until tender, then blend with the nut milk and herbs. Put the soup in a saucepan and heat to almost boiling on medium heat. (Do not boil or overheat!) Serve immediately.

This is a wonderful, creamy soup, more flavourful than some soups made with cow's milk, as the dairy milk actually detracts from the flavour of the vegetables.

Keeps 3–5 days refrigerated. Do not freeze.

Cream of Zucchini (or Broccoli) Soup
(Serves 2–4)

3	small zucchini *or* broccoli stalks (12–14 oz.), finely chopped
½–¾ cup	green onion tops, finely chopped
2 Tbs	butter
2 Tbs	whole wheat flour *or* other flour
½ tsp	sea salt
1¼ cups	milk
1 cup	cream

In 1 Tbs of the melted butter, sauté the zucchini (or broccoli) until tender. Then puree the zucchini, green onion, milk, and sea salt in a food processor or blender.

Melt the other 1 Tbs butter and brown the flour in the butter for a couple of minutes on medium heat. Mix the zucchini mixture with the browned flour and heat it in a saucepan on low heat until hot but not boiling. Keep covered. Remove from heat, stir in the cream, heat to almost boiling on low, and serve hot. Garnish with extra chopped green onions or chives.

Keeps 2–3 days refrigerated. Do not freeze.

Green Celery Soup

(Serves 6–8)

2 cups	chopped white potato (about 1 very large), with skin
3 cups	chopped celery
2 cups	water *or* light stock
1	large onion, chopped
1 Tbs	butter *or* cold-pressed oil
¼ cup	chopped fresh parsley
2 Tbs	tamari soy sauce
1	vegetable bouillon cube
1 tsp	vegetable broth powder
¾–1 tsp	sea salt
¼ tsp	paprika
	Cayenne pepper to taste
2 cups	celery, chopped
½ cup	water
⅓–½ cup	celery leaves, lightly chopped

Rinse the chopped potato thoroughly to remove excess starch. Simmer the potatoes with the 3 cups celery in the 2 cups water or stock, until tender. While these are cooking, sauté the onion in the oil or butter until slightly transparent. Blend all the ingredients *except* the remaining 2 cups celery, ½ cup water and celery leaves. In the original simmering pot, simmer the celery and water separately from the other ingredients until the celery is somewhat tender. Add the blended mixture to the simmered vegetables, along with the celery leaves. Stir and simmer everything together on low heat until hot enough to enjoy and serve. A unique and delicious soup! Keeps 3–5 days refrigerated. Do not freeze.

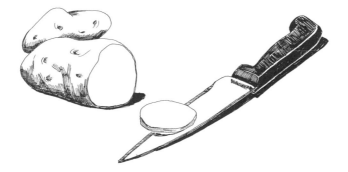

Cream of Celery Soup
(Serves 4–6)

5 cups	celery, chopped in ¼" moons
1 cup	water
1 cup	half-and-half *or* ⅓ cup cream and ⅔ cup milk*
1–2 Tbs	tamari soy sauce
2–4 tsp	white onion, chopped
2	vegetable bouillon cubes
1 tsp	vegetable broth powder
Few dashes each:	cayenne pepper and sea kelp
	Vegetable sea salt to taste

Simmer the chopped celery in 1 cup water for 5–8 minutes until fairly tender. Remove 1 cup of the steamed celery and set it aside. Blend the remaining 4 cups of celery and the leftover water with the half-and-half and all the remaining ingredients until liquefied. Put the blended mixture back into the simmering pot with the 1 cup sliced celery and bring them up to a low bubble on medium-low heat. Once it starts to simmer, turn the temperature to low and heat for 8–15 minutes until the flavours mingle. *Stock or milk substitute may be substituted for cream/milk with some loss of flavour. Correct seasonings to taste. Keeps refrigerated 4–6 days. Do not freeze.

French Green Bean Soup

(Serves 6–8)

2–4 Tbs	butter *or* cold-pressed oil
2 bunches	(about 16–20) green onions, chopped
1	795 mL (28 oz.) can of tomatoes with juice, cored and chopped, *or* 4–6 large tomatoes, chopped and 8–10 oz extra tomato juice
4 cups	(about 2 lbs.) fresh green beans, cut on a slant ¼" thick
8–10 oz	tomato juice
½ cup	water *or* stock
2	bay leaves (remove after soup is finished cooking)
2–3 Tbs	tamari soy sauce
2 Tbs	dried parsley *or* ⅓ cup chopped fresh parsley
2 tsp	basil
1 tsp	vegetable broth powder
1 tsp	paprika
1 tsp	vegetable sea salt

In a medium soup pot sauté the green onions in the butter or oil for 2–3 minutes. Add the tomatoes, juice, beans, bay leaves and water and simmer everything on medium-low heat for 20–30 minutes until the beans are very tender. Then add the remaining ingredients and cook everything together for an additional 15–25 minutes so the flavours can develop. A very flavourful, unique soup. Keeps 5–7 days refrigerated. May be frozen though it is best if it is not.

Cabbage Tomato Soup

5 cups	chopped green *or* savoy cabbage, cut in 1″ or slightly larger chunks
1 cup	water *or* stock
1	795 mL (28 oz) can of tomatoes, cored and chopped, *or* 4–6 large tomatoes, cored and chopped
1	10 oz (284 mL) can of tomato juice
1–2 Tbs	tamari soy sauce
1½ tsp	vegetable broth powder
¼ tsp	sea kelp
Few dashes	cayenne pepper
	Vegetable sea salt to taste
1 bunch	whole green onions (6–10), chopped small
1½ Tbs	oil *or* butter

Simmer the cabbage in water or stock for 5–7 minutes until a bit tender but still a little firm. Add the tomatoes and tomato juice and simmer another 15 minutes on low heat. While the vegetables are cooking, sauté the chopped green and white onions in the oil or butter for 1–2 minutes until lightly browned and tender. Add the onions with remaining oil or butter and all the other ingredients to the cabbage-tomato mixture, and cook everything on very low heat another 10 minutes or so until the flavours mingle. Correct the seasonings as desired. Keeps 5–7 days refrigerated. Do not freeze.

Cabbage Tomato Soup with Rice

Follow the directions for Cabbage Tomato Soup (above), but add 1–2 cups pre-cooked brown rice during the last 10 minutes of cooking time and use 2–3 Tbs of tamari soy sauce instead of the 1–2 Tbs. Use 2 bunches of green onions instead of one and correct the seasonings according to taste.

n of Cabbage Mushroom Soup
4)

4 cups	chopped green *or* savoy cabbage, cut in 1" or slightly larger chunks
1 cup	water *or* clear stock
1	medium onion, chopped small
2 cups	mushrooms, chopped
2 Tbs	butter
1 cup	half-and-half *or* milk
2	vegetable bouillon cubes
2 Tbs	whole wheat flour *or* other flour
½ tsp	paprika
¼ tsp	sea salt or to taste

Simmer the cabbage in water or stock for 7–9 minutes until a bit tender but still a little firm. Sauté the onion in the butter until clear, then add the mushrooms and sauté 1–2 minutes longer. Add these vegetables to the soup. Blend the remaining ingredients and seasonings in the blender, then add them to the cabbage-mushroom mixture and simmer everything together for another 10–14 minutes until the soup thickens a bit. Enjoy hot with parsley or chopped green onion tops as a garnish. Keeps 3–6 days refrigerated. Do not freeze.

Cream of Tomato Soup
(Serves 8–10)

9–12	large tomatoes, peeled, cored, seeded and finely chopped *or* 2 28-oz (795 mL) cans of tomatoes and their juice: core and crush the tomatoes and strain the juice
⅔ cup	celery (about 2 stalks), chopped
1	small onion, chopped
3 Tbs	unrefined, cold-pressed oil
1–2 tsp	tamari soy sauce
1 tsp	honey *or* other sweetener
½ tsp each	sea salt and paprika
Several dashes	cayenne pepper
Several dashes	sea kelp
Optional:	1–2 fresh tomatoes, peeled and chopped (if canned tomatoes are used)

1½ cups	milk *or* milk substitute

Sauté the onion and celery in the oil until slightly tender. Add the tomatoes and simmer on low heat, covered, for 30–40 minutes until the tomatoes are very tender and no longer taste acidic. Then add the herbs and remaining ingredients (except the milk) and cook another 10–15 minutes.

Cool the mixture slightly and blend it with the milk, using less milk for a richer, redder soup and more for a milder, creamier soup. Heat the soup to just before boiling point and serve hot, garnished with fresh parsley, green onions or chives.

Keeps refrigerated for 5–7 days. Avoid freezing.

Tomato Soup with Water: Use 1½ cups water (or nut milk) instead of real milk for a redder, more "tomatoey" soup.

Dilled Tomato Soup: Add ½–1 tsp dill weed to the blender mixture and a few dashes extra cayenne pepper.

Tomato-Rice Soup: Add ½–1 cup pre-cooked brown rice to the soup during the last heating. Add a few dashes extra sea salt and cayenne pepper. Adjust seasonings.

Carrot and Beet Soup (Mock Tomato Soup)

(Serves 4–5)

5	large carrots, sliced (about 4½ cups)
1	medium or 2 small beets, chopped (about 1 cup)
3–4	green onions, white parts only, chopped
2 cups	nut milk *or* milk
2 Tbs	tamari soy sauce
1–2 tsp	honey *or* maple syrup
1	vegetable bouillon cube
¼–½ tsp	vegetable sea salt or to taste
Several dashes	cayenne pepper
Couple dashes	sea kelp

Use very fresh beets, not storage beets, or the soup will taste old and bitter. Steam the beets and carrots until tender, about 10–15 minutes. Blend the vegetables with all the remaining ingredients and simmer everything in a saucepan for 10–15 minutes until the flavours blend. Serve hot and enjoy. Keeps 3–6 days refrigerated. Do not freeze.

Creamy Red Bell Pepper Soup (Mock Tomato Soup)

(Serves 4)

4	medium red bell peppers, chopped
1	medium parsnip, chopped (about 1 cup)
8-12	green onion tips, white part only, chopped
1 cup	half-and-half *or* ⅓ cup cream and ⅔ cup milk*
2-3 Tbs	butter *or* oil
2	vegetable bouillon cubes
Optional:	Few dashes cayenne pepper to taste
Optional:	Bit of sea salt (if unsalted butter or bouillon cubes are used)

Sauté the peppers, parsnip and onions in the butter or oil until very tender. Blend all the ingredients thoroughly and then strain them into a saucepan. Heat the soup until hot throughout and serve. The soup looks and tastes a bit like cream of tomato soup. The flavour is fabulous. *If a milk substitute is desired for this recipe add 1-2 tsp liquid sweetening and correct the seasonings, as milk adds a lot to the flavour of this soup.

Keeps 3-5 days refrigerated. Do not freeze.

Cream of Cauliflower Soup
(Serves 4–6)

2 cups	milk *or* substitute*
3 cups	cauliflower, chopped into small pieces
1 cup	white potato (about 1 medium), peeled and chopped into small pieces
½	small onion, chopped
2 Tbs	butter
½ tsp	sea salt
¼ tsp	paprika
Few dashes	cayenne pepper
2	stalks celery, cut into 2–3 long strips each and finely chopped
1 Tbs	extra butter
2 Tbs	white rice miso *or* ½ tsp extra sea salt

Sauté the onion in the 2 Tbs butter in a 2-litre (or 2-quart) saucepan until tender and slightly transparent. Steam the cauliflower and potato until tender in a separate pot. Put the onion, cauliflower, and potato in the blender or food processor and liquefy.

Use the saucepan to sauté the celery in 1 Tbs butter until very tender, and remove it from the heat. Add the blended mixture to the saucepan, and heat it on low to medium heat to boiling point, but do not boil. Stir in the extra sea salt, or remove 2 cups of the liquid from the soup and carefully mix in the miso so there are no lumps. Then re-add the liquid to the soup and remove from the heat.

Serve as is or garnish with chopped, fresh parsley or alfalfa sprouts. This is a hearty, thick, and filling soup. Keeps 4–5 days refrigerated. Do not freeze.

*Instead of milk, 1¾ cups thick nut milk and ¼ cup butter may be used.

Potato Soup

(Serves 6)

4 cups	white potatoes, unpeeled, chopped into very small cubes
2 Tbs	unrefined, cold-pressed oil
1	medium onion, very finely chopped
2–3	cloves garlic, minced
1 cup	water *or* clear vegetable stock
2	vegetable bouillon cubes
2½ cups	milk *or* substitute
4 Tbs	butter
½ tsp each	sea salt and paprika
Several dashes	cayenne pepper
Optional:	Several dashes dry mustard
2 Tbs	white rice miso *or* ½ tsp extra sea salt

Steam the potatoes until tender. In a small soup pot, sauté the onion and garlic in oil until tender. Then add the water and bouillon cubes and simmer until the cubes dissolve completely, stirring occasionally.

While the bouillon is simmering, blend or process 3 of the 4 cups of potatoes with the milk, butter, and remaining ingredients (except the miso). Add the blended mixture and the extra 1 cup of steamed potatoes to the onion and bouillon, and after mixing, simmer on very low heat for about 10 minutes until the flavours mingle and the soup is hot. Do not boil.

If miso is used, remove 1 cup of the soup and mix

the miso into it, then return it to the soup before serving. Serve the soup garnished with chopped green onions or chives.

Keeps 5–6 days refrigerated. Do not freeze.

Dilled Potato Soup: Add 2 tsp dill weed and 1 chopped green onion to the blender mixture.

Curried Potato Soup: Add 1½–2 tsp curry powder, 1 tsp tumeric, and 1 tsp honey or other sweetener to the blended mixture. *Optional:* 1 cup peas, added to the bouillon mixture.

Leek and Potato Soup
(Serves 8-10)

4-5	leeks (about 2 lbs)
2½ cups	water
1 cup	milk
2	medium potatoes, unpeeled, chopped (about 2½-2¾ cups), rinsed thoroughly before cooking
1½ cups	water
1 cup	cream
½ cup	milk
3 Tbs	tamari soy sauce
2-4 Tbs	butter *or* cold-pressed oil
2	vegetable bouillon cubes
1 tsp	paprika
Several dashes	cayenne pepper and sea kelp
	Vegetable sea salt to taste

Wash the leeks carefully and trim about ½-1" off the green tops and discard. Remove all the green tops from the white bases of the leeks except for about the bottom 1" of green. Chop the green part very fine and simmer it in the 2½ cups water on low heat, covered, for 60-70 minutes until very tender.

Blend the leek greens and remaining water with the 1 cup milk and set aside. Now simmer the chopped leek whites and potatoes in the additional 1½ cups water for 12-18 minutes until tender. Blend the leek whites and potatoes with all the remaining ingredients. Add this mixture to the leek greens mixture in a medium-large soup pot and stir them together with a wire whisk. Cover the soup and let it simmer on low heat until hot throughout. A bit of the raw, white, chopped leek can be added to the blended mixture before simmering for added texture and flavour if desired. Serve and enjoy this satisfying soup within 3–6 days. Do not freeze.

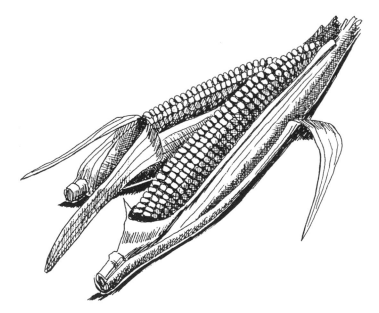

Parsnip Soup

(Serves 4-6)

4 cups	firm, white parsnips, chopped
1 cup	fresh, unblemished, small parsnip tips, cut in rounds
2½-3½ cups	water, light stock, milk *or* milk substitute
2-5	green onion tips, white part only, chopped
1-2 Tbs	butter *or* oil
3-5 tsp	light miso
½ tsp	sea salt
¼-½ tsp	cinnamon
¼ tsp	nutmeg

Steam the 4 cups of parsnips until tender. Blend the steamed parsnips with all the remaining ingredients *except* the parsnip tips. Steam or sauté the remaining parsnips in extra oil or butter, until they are tender. Simmer everything together on low heat until hot throughout. Correct spices if desired. Serve and enjoy.

Keeps 2-4 days refrigerated. Do not freeze.

Pumpkin or Squash Soup Almondine
(Serves 4–6)

½	small onion, finely chopped
1 Tbs	unrefined, cold-pressed oil
2 cups	cooked pumpkin, butternut *or* buttercup squash
1½–2 cups	thick nut milk (blanched almond nut milk is best)
4 Tbs	butter
1 tsp each	sea salt and cinnamon
¼ tsp each	ginger and nutmeg
½ tsp	ground cloves

Garnish: ½ cup raw slivered almonds, "home-roasted" and hot

The pumpkin or squash may be boiled whole or cut in pieces and baked at 400° until tender (about 1–1½ hours) for use in this recipe. Do not use any other squash as they are not tender or sweet enough for this soup.

Sauté the onion in the oil and then blend it with the remaining ingredients. Heat the soup in a large saucepan on very low heat until hot throughout. Stir often. Serve this soup in small portions as it is very rich. Garnish each serving with the roasted almonds, or use pecans if almonds are unavailable.

Keeps refrigerated for 5–7 days. This soup is best if not frozen. (See recipe for "Home-Roasted" Nuts.)

Carrot Soup
(Serves 4)

4 cups	carrots, slivered and steamed until tender
1⅔ cups	vegetable steaming water *or* vegetable stock
2–3 Tbs	butter *or* 1–2 Tbs unrefined, cold-pressed oil
2 Tbs	tamari soy sauce
2 tsp	parsley
1 tsp	dill weed *or* tarragon, crushed
½ tsp	sea salt
Several dashes	sea kelp
	Cayenne pepper to taste
Optional:	1 tsp fresh onion *or* garlic, crushed, *or* ¼ tsp onion or garlic powder *or* a few crushed, dried or fresh mint leaves

Liquefy all ingredients until smooth in a blender or food processor. Then heat the soup in a saucepan on low-to-medium heat just up to boiling. Do not boil. Serve hot, garnished with chopped chives, green onions or chopped fresh parsley if desired.

Will keep 3–5 days refrigerated. Do not freeze.

Garlic and Greens Soup
(Serves 4)

10–12	medium large garlic cloves, sliced
¼ cup	butter *or* 2 Tbs butter and 2 Tbs unrefined cold-pressed oil

4	large garlic cloves, pressed
4 cups	water *or* stock
4–5	green onion tops (green part only), finely chopped
½–1	bunch spinach
¼ cup	tomato juice
1–2 Tbs	parsley
1 tsp	vegetized sea salt
½ tsp	sea kelp
3–4 Tbs	dark miso
Optional:	Parmesan cheese, croutons

Sauté the garlic slices in the butter or butter/oil mixture on low to medium heat until thoroughly browned. Remove and discard the garlic. Add the water and the remaining ingredients except the miso and the optional ingredients. Simmer 20–25 minutes. Remove 1 cup of liquid from the soup and stir the miso into it until it is completely dissolved, then re-add the liquid to the soup and stir.

This robust yet light soup is very healing and strengthening. It is especially good for colds and flus. When not used for medicinal purposes, it may be served with croutons or crusty bread and sprinkled with parmesan cheese.

Best if eaten within 3–5 days. Do not freeze.

Chilled Summer Soups

Gazpacho
(Serves 6-8)

1	large can or jar (48 oz or 1.36 L) tomato juice
2-4	peeled tomatoes, chopped
1	medium cucumber (organic is best), peeled, seeded and chopped
1	medium green pepper, chopped
6-8	green onions (white part only), chopped
2	cloves garlic, minced
2 tsp	basil
½ tsp	sea salt *or* ½-1 tsp vegetized sea salt
½ tsp	cayenne pepper (or less)
Optional:	1 cup sour cream *or* yogurt

Thoroughly blend all the ingredients except the optional sour cream or yogurt. Lastly, add the sour cream or yogurt, if desired, and blend only a few more seconds. Chill for preferably 2 hours and serve cold. Garnish with chopped green onion tops or chives.

Keeps 2-3 days refrigerated. Do not freeze.

Cucumber Yogurt Soup
(Serves 4-6)

4 cups	cucumber, peeled, seeded and chopped
2 cups	yogurt
¼ cup	water *or* ice cubes
6-8	green onion tops (green part only), chopped
2	cloves garlic, minced
8-10	fresh mint leaves (in a pinch use ½-1 tsp dried)
1 tsp	sea salt
½-1 tsp	dill weed

Blend everything and chill for about 2 hours or more. Garnish with unpeeled, thinly sliced cucumber rounds or chopped fresh parsley. Keeps 2-3 days refrigerated. Do not freeze.

Cold Tomato Zucchini Soup
(Serves 4)

4	large tomatoes, chopped, *or* 1 795-mL (28 oz) can tomatoes, cored, chopped and excess juice drained *except* for ½ cup
1 cup	yogurt
2–4	green onions, chopped
1–2	cloves garlic, minced
1 Tbs	lemon juice
½–1 tsp	vegetable sea salt or to taste
Several dashes	cayenne pepper
Optional:	1–2 Tbs chopped fresh parsley
1	medium zucchini, grated (about 1½ cups)

Blend all ingredients except the zucchini. Chill for 1–2 hours and then add the fresh grated zucchini, mix with a spoon and then serve. Garnish with extra chopped green onion tops or chives.

Keeps 2–3 days refrigerated. Do not freeze.

Cold Red Bell Pepper Soup

(Serves 2–4)

2	medium red bell peppers, chopped (about 2 cups)
1 cup	yogurt
2	green onions, white part only, chopped
¼ tsp	sea salt
Optional:	Couple dashes cayenne pepper
1	small or medium red bell pepper, chopped small
1 cup	alfalfa sprouts *or* other sprouts *or* grated zucchini

Blend the first five ingredients in the blender, thoroughly. Strain and chill the mixture if desired. Mix the extra chopped red pepper into the soup and top each bowl with a handful of sprouts. Serve and enjoy.

Keeps 2–3 days refrigerated. Do not freeze.

Cold Avocado Soup
(Serves 2–4)

1	large or 2 small ripe avocados
1 cup	yogurt
½ cup	water
2–3 tsp	white onion, chopped
½ tsp	vegetable broth powder
¼–½ tsp	curry powder
Couple dashes	each: cayenne pepper and sea kelp
	Vegetable sea salt *or* other mixed herb seasonings, to taste
Optional:	1–2 tsp tamari soy sauce

Peel the avocados and place them in a blender or food processor to liquefy. Add the remaining ingredients. Adjust the seasonings to suit individual tastes if desired. This lovely green soup keeps 1–4 days refrigerated if kept tightly covered in a glass container. Do not freeze.

Mock Vichyssoise (Cold Potato Soup)

(Serves 4)

4 cups	unpeeled, cubed white potatoes
½ cup	water *or* clear stock
1 cup	half-and-half *or* ⅓ cup cream and ⅔ cup milk
1	vegetable bouillon cube
¼ tsp	sea salt, or a bit more to taste
Dash or two	cayenne pepper

1 Tbs	butter
1 bunch	green onions (about 6–10), white part only, chopped

Green onion tops, chopped

Scrub the potatoes with a vegetable brush, cut them into small cubes and rinse them several times to remove excess starch. Simmer them in the water or stock for about 10 minutes until tender. Blend the potatoes and any remaining cooking water with the half-and-half, bouillon cube, salt and pepper. In a small skillet heat the butter and sauté the finely chopped onion whites for 1–2 minutes until lightly browned and very tender. Add the onion and butter to the rest of the blended mixture and blend again. Add a dash more sea salt or vegetable sea salt if desired. Chill the soup thoroughly and serve hot or cold, garnished with a sprinkling of chopped green onions. Keeps 3–5 days. Do not freeze.

Hearty Stews

"When a soup is too light, a stew is just right."

An identifying characteristic of most soups is an abundance of broth or creamy liquid that may compose as much as fifty percent or more of the soup. The chunky or solid ingredients in the soup are generally less in amount by comparison.

Stews generally are composed of vegetables, noodles, beans, grains, (and traditionally meat) with a little liquid or gravy surrounding them for added flavour. Most of the guidelines for soups also apply to stews.

Stews may often be served all by themselves as a meal, or alongside or over: rice, whole grains, mashed potatoes, squash, noodles, crusty bread or other starchy foods. Stews are convenient and usually store, freeze and travel well. They are an easy one-step meal.

Hearty stews are especially satisfying in winter but these vegetarian stews are a treat any time of year. Include them in lunchboxes, on camping trips or for quick dinners. Stews provide a substantial, wholesome feeling and are a nourishing part of a meal.

Hearty Stew Recipes

Ratatouille Stew (Mediterranean)
(Serves 4-6)

1	large onion, chopped
4-6	cloves garlic, minced
1	medium eggplant, peeled and chopped in small pieces
1 cup	tomato juice
¼ cup	unrefined, cold-pressed oil
2	bay leaves (remove before serving)
2 Tbs	dried parsley
1 ½ tsp	sea salt
1 tsp each	basil, marjoram and oregano
⅛ tsp	rosemary
	Cayenne pepper to taste
3-4	medium tomatoes, in small chunks
2	large green peppers, sliced in thin strips
2	medium zucchini, in chunks
3 Tbs	tomato paste
Garnish:	fresh chopped parsley, green onions *or* chives

Heat the oil in a large pot, and sauté the onion and garlic on fairly high heat until slightly tender. Add the eggplant, lightly salt it, and continue to sauté until the eggplant is semi-tender and the onions and garlic are fairly transparent. Now add the tomato juice and herbs, stir, cover and simmer on low heat for 12–15 minutes until the eggplant is very tender. Add the peppers and zucchini, tomatoes and tomato paste. (The tomatoes may be added earlier with the eggplant if more tender tomatoes are desired.)

Stir and simmer 5–10 minutes more until the new vegetables are somewhat tender but still retain a bit of crunchiness, or are as tender as you like. It can be topped with suggested toppings and served by itself or over a bed of brown rice, couscous, another whole grain or over steamed cauliflower.

Keeps refrigerated 5–7 days. Do not freeze. Delicious!

Sweet and Sour Lentil Stew
(Serves 3–4)

> 2–2½ cups water
> 1 cup dry brown lentils
> 1 small onion, finely chopped
> 3–4 Tbs apple cider vinegar
> 3–4 Tbs honey (use same amount as vinegar)
> 1 Tbs unrefined, cold-pressed oil
> 1 tsp sea salt
> 1 tsp basil

Bring the water and lentils to a boil on high heat and immediately turn the heat to low so the lentils are bubbling gently. Cook them covered for about ½ hour, add the onions and cook another 15 minutes.

After 45 minutes, if most of the water is not cooked out or absorbed by the lentils, remove the lid of the pan and let the lentils finish cooking for 15–25 minutes more until most of the liquid is gone and the lentils are fully cooked and very tender. Then add the oil and remaining ingredients. Cook the lentils, covered, for another 5–8 minutes or so until the flavour of the spices mingles with them.

When finished cooking, the lentils should look like a very thick soup or stew. Serve hot or cold by itself or over brown rice, millet, or another whole grain. Great for lunchboxes.

Keeps 7–8 days refrigerated and may be frozen if necessary.

A few stalks of chopped celery may also be added for extra flavour and colour.

Curried Red Lentil Stew (East Indian)

(Serves 4–6)

3–4 cups	water
1 cup	red lentils
1	onion, finely chopped
1 cup	fresh or frozen peas
2 Tbs	butter (*or* 1 Tbs unrefined, cold-pressed oil)
2–3 tsp	honey *or* other sweetener
2 tsp	curry powder
1 tsp each	sea salt and tumeric
⅛–¼ tsp each	cayenne pepper, cominos (ground cumin) and coriander
Several dashes	cinnamon
Several dashes	ground cloves
1–2 cups	cauliflower, chopped into small flowerets

Begin cooking the lentils, onion, and peas in the water. In a separate pan, steam the cauliflower until tender. Red lentils will take 15–20 minutes to cook fully. Do not overcook them or they will fall apart. Cook only until tender.

When the lentils are tender, yet still a little firm, add the spices, cauliflower, butter, and sweetening, and cook everything together an additional 5–10 minutes so the flavours can mingle. Correct the spices according to personal taste. Add extra water if necessary so the legumes will be contained in sauce. Enjoy with brown rice, millet, barley or another whole grain.

Keeps refrigerated for 5–7 days. May be frozen.

Kidney Bean Stew

(Serves 12–14)

2½ cups	dry kidney beans, soaked and cooked
1 lb	carrots (about 7–8 medium), sliced in ⅓ to ½ inch chunks
½–1 lb	mushrooms (2½–5 cups), halved or quartered
8–10	stalks celery, sliced in 1-inch chunks
6	medium potatoes, chopped in 1-inch chunks
3–4	medium onions, chopped
2–3	green peppers *or* 2 small zucchini, cut in chunks
1–2 cups	fresh or frozen corn and/or peas
Optional:	1–2 cups chopped broccoli *or* cauliflower
Optional:	6–10 Jerusalem artichokes
2–3 Tbs	tamari soy sauce
2 Tbs	vegetable broth powder *or* 3–4 vegetable bouillon cubes
2–3 Tbs	parsley
1½ tsp	sea salt
1 tsp each	sea kelp and basil
½ tsp	paprika
⅛ tsp or less	cayenne pepper
Optional:	⅛ tsp *each* cumin powder and thyme

Read the tips at the beginning of this book on preparing bean soups (page 3). While the beans are cooking and nearly finished, steam the hard vegetables, potatoes, artichokes, carrots, cauliflower, and broccoli (if any), in a separate pot for 10–15 minutes. When the beans are done, drain off all except 2 cups of cooking water. Then add the pre-cooked and other vegetables along with the herbs and remaining ingredients.

Simmer everything together on low to medium heat for 20–25 minutes until the flavours mingle. Serve hot along with a crusty bread.

Will keep about 7 days refrigerated and freezes well. Hearty and delicious!

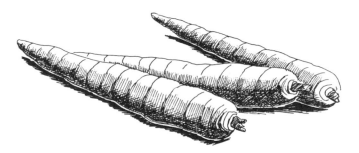

Tangy Vegetable Stew

(Serves 1–2)

1	onion, chopped
1–2	cloves garlic, minced
1	small zucchini, sliced in ¼-inch rounds
1	green pepper, cut into thin strips
½–1 cup	broccoli *or* cauliflower, chopped
½–1 cup	mushrooms, sliced or chopped
3–4	large tomatoes, chopped *or* 1 medium or large can tomatoes, drained and chopped
2–4 Tbs	oil
2–3 oz	tomato paste or ½ a small can
½ tsp each	sea salt, cumin powder, coriander and chili powder
Several dashes	cayenne pepper

Sauté all the vegetables except the tomatoes in the oil until tender. Add the tomatoes and remaining ingredients and sauté for several more minutes. Serve over brown rice, millet, another grain or over steamed cauliflower. A quick and tasty meal to serve in a hurry for 1 or 2 people. It also reheats easily in a saucepan.

Variations:

Garnish with black olives, avocado slices or alfalfa sprouts.

Serve the vegetables on a bed of mung bean sprouts or fresh chopped spinach.

Add red bell pepper strips, corn, peas, carrots or another vegetable to the vegetables that are sautéed.

Add ½ cup or less fresh parsley, chopped, to the recipe.

Serve the vegetables over hot polenta (cornmeal mixed with grated cheddar cheese).

Serve over coked couscous, barley, buckwheat, kasha, wheat berries (kernels), bulgur, quinoa or another unusual grain.

Serve with big chunks of cornbread, whole wheat or other whole grain bread or with corn chips.

Incredible Chili

[Serves 6–8]

2½ cups	dry kidney beans, soaked and cooked
2	medium onions, chopped (about 2 cups)
12–13 oz	tomato paste
4–5	large tomatoes *or* 1 795 mL (28 oz) can tomatoes, cored and chopped
4–6	cloves garlic, minced
2–4 Tbs	oil
2–3 Tbs	tamari soy sauce
3 tsp	chili powder
2 tsp	parsley
1–1½ tsp	sea salt
1 tsp	oregano
1 tsp	crushed red peppers *or* 1–2 fresh hot peppers, chopped
½ tsp	sea kelp (important)
¼ tsp	cumin seeds *or* ½ tsp cumin powder (cominos)
¹⁄₁₆ –¼ tsp	cayenne pepper
Optional:	1 green pepper, chopped

While the kidney beans are cooking, heat the oil in a large skillet and sauté the onions and garlic for 2–3 minutes. Then add the green peppers, if any, and sauté another 1–2 minutes. Add the tomatoes and simmer for another 10–15 minutes. All the remaining ingredients can be added next. Simmer the sauce on low heat for 35–50 minutes to develop the flavour.

When the beans are ready, drain them and save the liquid. Mix the sauce and beans together and add some of the reserved bean liquid if needed to bring the chili to the desired consistency. Cook the chili for 15–25 minutes so the sauce flavour mingles with the beans. Serve hot or cool and store. Keeps refrigerated for 7 days or may be frozen. Note: The amount of cayenne determines the "hotness" of the chili.

Serve over brown rice or another whole grain, with chunks or bread or cornbread or with yogurt, avocado or grated cheese. For a chili soup, add 1 cup or more tomato juice for a more soup-like consistency, and correct the seasonings as desired.

Index

A

Aduki soup, 23
Almondine, pumpkin
 or squash soup, 68
Apple cider vinegar,
 13
Arrowroot powder,
 7, 11
Asparagus soup,
 cream of, 42
Avocado soup, cold,
 75

B

Bean soup, aduki, 23
Bean soup, black, 25
Bean soup,
 fasoulada, 27
Bean soup, green and
 red mung, 29
Bean soup, hearty
 mung, 28
Bean soup, pinto, 23
Bean soups,
 preparing, 3
Bean stew, kidney, 82

Beans, 9
Beans, canned, 13
Beet soup, carrot and
 (Mock tomato
 soup), 59
Black bean soup, 25
Borscht, 39
Broccoli or zucchini
 soup, 47
Broccoli or zucchini
 soup, cream of, 48
Butter, 10–11

C

Cabbage mushroom
 soup, cream of, 56
Cabbage tomato
 soup, 54
Cabbage tomato soup
 with rice, 55
Carrot and beet soup
 (Mock tomato
 soup), 59
Carrot soup, 69
Cauliflower soup,
 cream of, 61

Cayenne pepper, 8, 12
Celery soup, cream
  of, 52
Celery soup, green,
  50
Chili, incredible, 86
Cold avocado soup,
  75
Cold red bell pepper
  soup, 74
Cold tomato zucchini
  soup, 73
Corn chowder, 41
Cornstarch, 11
Cream, 7, 11
Cream of asparagus
  soup, 42
Cream of cabbage
  mushroom soup, 56
Cream of cauliflower
  soup, 61
Cream of celery
  soup, 52
Cream of tomato
  soup, 57
Creamy red bell
  pepper soup (Mock
  tomato soup), 60
Cucumber yogurt
  soup, 72
Curried potato soup,
  64
Curried red lentil

stew (East Indian),
  81

D

Dilled potato soup, 64
Dilled tomato soup,
  58
Dried mushroom
  soup, 38

E

Easy miso soup, 21
Eggplant, 12

F

Fasoulada Bean
  Soup, 27
Flour, 7
  amaranth, 11
  barley, 11
  buckwheat, 11
  corn, 11
  millet, 11
  oat, 11
  white, 11
  whole wheat, 11
French green bean
  soup, 53

G

Garlic, 9
Garlic and Greens
  soup, 70

Gazpacho, 71
Green and red mung
    bean soup, 29
Green bean soup,
    French, 53
Green celery soup, 50
Greens soup, garlic
    and, 70

H
Hearty mung bean
    soup, 28
Herbs, 7, 11–12, 14
Home-roasted nuts,
    47
Honey, 11

I
Incredible chili, 86

K
Kale soup, 45
Kidney bean stew, 82

L
Leek and potato
    soup, 65
Lentil soup, 30
Lentil stew, curried
    red (East Indian),
    81
Lentil stew, sweet
    and sour, 80

Lentil tomato soup,
    31
Lentils, 9

M
Malt, 11
Maple syrup, 11
Meat bones, 11
Meat juices, 11
Milk, 7, 11
Milk substitutes, 11,
    46
Minestrone soup, 34
Miso, 6, 11–12, 14
Miso soup, 22
Miso soup, easy, 21
Mock tomato soup,
    59–60
Mock vichyssoise, 76
Molasses, 11
Mung bean soup,
    green and red, 29
Mung bean soup,
    hearty, 28
Mushroom cabbage
    soup, cream of, 56
Mushroom soup, 37
Mushroom soup,
    dried, 38
Mushrooms, 12

N
Nut milk, 46

O

Oil, 10–11, 14
Onion soup, 36
Onions, 9

P

Parsley soup, 44
Parsnip soup, 67
Pea soup, split, 32
Peas, 9
Pepper, black, 12
Pepper, cayenne, 8, 12
Pinto bean soup, 23
Potato soup, 63
Potato soup, curried, 64
Potato soup, dilled, 64
Potato soup, leek and, 65
Pumpkin or squash soup almondine, 68

Q

Quick Sip, 12, 15

R

Ratatouille stew (Mediterranean), 78
Red bell pepper soup, cold, 74

Red bell pepper soup, creamy (Mock tomato soup), 60
Red lentil stew (East Indian), curried, 81
Rice soup, Tomato-, 58
Rice, Cabbage tomato soup with, 55

S

Salt, 12
Salt substitutes, 14
Sea kelp, 6, 11
Sea salt, 6, 12
Seaweed, 15
Spices, 8
Spinach soup, 43
Split pea soup, 32
Squash or pumpkin soup almondine, 68
Substitutions chart, 11
Sugar, 11
Sugar, raw, 11
Sweet and Sour Lentil Stew, 80
Sweeteners, 7, 11

T

Tamari soy sauce, 6, 11–12, 15

Tangy vegetable
stew, 84
Tomato soup with
rice, cabbage, 55
Tomato soup with
water, 58
Tomato soup,
cabbage, 54
Tomato soup, cream
of, 57
Tomato soup, dilled,
58
Tomato soup, lentil, 31
Tomato soup, mock,
59
Tomato soup,
vegetable, 17
Tomato zucchini
soup, cold, 73
Tomato-rice soup, 58

V

Vegetable bouillon
cubes, 7, 11, 13
Vegetable broth, 18
Vegetable broth
powder, 7, 11, 16

Vegetable sea salt, 16
Vegetable soup, 19
Vegetable stew,
tangy, 84
Vegetable stock, 2, 7,
11
Vegetable tomato
soup, 17
Vegetables, dried, 16
Vichyssoise, mock,
76

W

Worcestershire
sauce, 12

Y

Yogurt cucumber
soup, 72

Z

Zucchini or broccoli
soup, 47
Zucchini or broccoli
soup, cream of, 48
Zucchini tomato
soup, cold, 73